“LMOAKJ”

(Learn More After Obstacles Kenneth’s Journey)

BY

KENNETH JON DIXON

Printed in the United States of America

ISBN-9781520503141

Connect with me on Twitter
@lmaoKJ

Table of Contents

CHAPTER 1

A Broke Man is an Optimist

On my road to success I always thought about my book getting in Big Sean's hand. He was my hero. I wanted him to read what I learned from him and how he changed my whole life around just by his music. I knew he'd be inspired but I had no idea of how I'd get it to him. I also wanted him to let Kanye West read it too. I was a big fan of the both of them. I thought about Kanye West's record label name, which is "Getting Out Our Dreams Good Music". I wanted to sign to Good Music (Kanye West's label) or Finally Famous (Big Sean's label.) I knew they both would've helped my book reach millions of people hands. I wasn't a rapper but I knew they'd feel where I was coming from and sign me. I remembered listening to Kanye West's verse on Blessings where he said "I was thinking about starting up my own school". Then I thought about my dream which was being a basketball coach. I wanted to be a coach for his school. We both inspire people and want the best for them. I became happier when I thought about what Big Sean said in one of his verses which was "Why don't schools teach more mathematics less trigonometry and more about taxes. They at the chalkboard teaching us ass backwards. How about preparing us for life instead of lab rat us". I knew that Kanye would listen to Big Sean's thoughts about the school. I knew it would be one of the best schools in America because Kanye is running for president in 2020!

I began to build up my mind, on believing that I'll have enough wealth to take care of my mom and sister. I began to think, "What if my book doesn't sell as many copies as I want it to?" I always thought

about the people who don't like to read and those who don't have the money to buy a copy. I began to start second guessing myself. Asking myself, "Is this book really worth it?" I knew it would change so many teens'
mindsets, yet I knew some would ignore it and continue doing bad. I always noticed when I started to second guess myself, subconsciously I forgot that God was with me the whole time. It became like a habit to me. Over time I began to break that habit by asking God to always remind me that He's with me. I would get distracted, that was one of my problems and it may be a problem for many others, as well. My family members sometimes get aggravated then get distracted and forget that God is always with them. They've been in church their whole lives but I noticed how they didn't work on improving themselves. Whenever they notice they had a big problem. I also noticed that you can do something your whole life but if you don't program your mind it will be programmed by the whole, meaning society, poor circumstances, feeling of inadequacy, etc.

A legend in the making, I'm now unstoppable. My mindset is built on growing more and more. I'm not yet satisfied with my results. I'know they are better than average but I also know that I can do more. I push myself to do more every day. As long as I've got God on my side all things are possible. But Jesus beheld [them], and said unto them, With men this is impossible; but with God all things are possible. - Matthew 19:26. I've come to realize that I will be okay. My main goal in life is to change teens' mindsets for the better. Many teens aren't able to do what's possible instead they focus on the impossible. I honestly believe that God is the key to life, especially when you're doing well in life. God has been blessing me tremendously, I experienced the Holy Spirit at an early age. I didn't know how to approach God at first but as I got older and had a personal relationship with him it came quite naturally. When I was dealing with misery at the age of 17 years old, I had no one to talk to but God, my mother, and my sister. I had no idea that I was hurting my mom. When my mom noticed how stressed out I was she sought help for me. At this point I didn't care about anything or anyone. Mother would always say, "What's the matter with you, Son? How can I help you get through this?" I didn't respond. I just knew for a fact that I wouldn't be able to get over the fact of my girlfriend leaving me. I didn't even know that my mother was praying for me but, I'm thankful that she did. I had no knowledge of how God was going to fix my situation but I'm a living testimony that He saw me through.

Most pray for success yet refuse to take action. I've always heard that a man who doesn't work doesn't eat. To me that's confirmation on doing my best and letting God do the rest. I noticed how many who are not where they want to be in life blame others because of certain situations in which people have hurt them. I blamed myself for my ex leaving me, it wasn't her fault. In the relationship when we fussed about leaving each other I should have been searching the web and reading books on how to overcome a breakup. I was so focused on how she always telling me that she would never leave me no matter what comes our way. I remember my brother said that a woman can build you up and she also can tear you down. I was a victim of a broken promise that I thought would hold fast. My mindset was too weak to look forward to moving on without her but, eventually, my family noticed how much I was stressing , would give me positive quotes that would build up my confidence like:

1 What doesn't kill you will make you stronger.
2 If it's meant to be it will be.
3 There are plenty of fish in the sea that are waiting on my net to drop.

Since my mentality was weak,I talked to my aunt who's been married for 20 years and she explained to me how some relationships are only meant for when you are young. She told me that most relationships are just practice for marriage. This also made me feel better. She told me how to give my problems to God and let them go. In my mind I was confused because when I usually pray I'll worry about the problem rather than letting Him fix it. I asked her, "How do you

cope with a problem?" and she responded, "If you are going to worry, don't pray, but if you pray, don't worry." The saying was so simple, I truly believed it
from then on. I called it "The Key To Praying Without Ceasing," so I continue to use that method which drew me closer to God.

The moment when you get over who hurt you, you'll replace all that sadness with success. I learned from The Great Frank Sinatra that the best revenge is success. It took me a long time to realize how that works. I just have faith in God that one day I'll make it. Over time I began to miss her even though she hurt me. I thought that she would never treat me that way that she did, but it happened. I reached out to her. I wanted to see if she really cared about me, but I got no response. It has been said that success is a lonely road. This makes me believe that everything happens for a reason. Eventually God removed her out of my way. My past instantly reminded me of when I told my ex that I would kill myself if she were to leave me. She then took my kindness for weakness. She fooled around with other guys and always asked me why couldn't I be a normal guy and move on. By her continuing to lead me on I thought we would be together forever. Even though I went through the worst state of depression from heartbreak, knowledge saved me. I heard the saying that; the harder the battle the sweeter the success. My mind was stuck on being alone all the time.

Approaching the end of the summer of 2015, my ex finally decided to leave me. I just graduated High School and I enrolled in college for the fall semester. My self-esteem was too low to go out and meet new girls. I figured that I'd just wait to see what the school year would bring on. Upon enrolling I turned in everything that I needed, yet I had another bump in the road. They hit me with the fact that I didn't pass a class called Physical Science. I was told that I can't start school until I get online and retake the course that I needed. So that left me to start school in January 2016.

The more you think about how people aggravate you the more you get aggravated. I had been trapped by this mental obstacle for a long time. By listening to music and learning facts like, you are what you think

about I've come to realize that it's always best to think positively because you'll eventually have positivity attracted to you. The Law of Attraction is the ability to attract into our lives whatever we are focusing on. Those sayings made me realize that if I continue to let this affect me it will affect me forever. Some folks lose their lives or take others' lives because they aggravated by other people. I began to keep my cool and realized that we aren't perfect. I began to separate myself from them in order to be alone. Then I started to feel better. I couldn't run from the aggravators forever, I knew eventually I had to get over it. I began to think about the law of attraction when it talks about when you are mad you are sending the same feelings to the universe. This made me come to my senses. I realized that if I continued to keep getting mad at people, the devil will eventually take control. I avoided that by going to God, asking Him to help with things that were beyond my control. Every time I saw myself getting mad at others I told myself will I be mad at them when I become successful? I came to realize that my future was more important than an argument.

Chapter 2

Realization of My Talent

I began to pray and ask God to help me stay focused on what was important, like getting the Physical Science class out of the way so I can start school. Many may have a relationship partner or a family member to help them stay focused on what's possible. I had no one to run to but God. It became a habit to me, in every problem or situation I ran to God. My faith was being built up by the "Key To Praying" so anything was possible. After every obstacle there was a blessing, such as lyrics from a gospel song that helped me get through the day, like "Imagine Me Being Free." This motivated me to continue to stay focused on what I wanted. I made it a must to keep God first at all times because I didn't want to lose the power of God. I stopped doing what I knew was wrong like cursing, smoking, and disrespecting others. I began to think that in the long run it would jeopardize my future. If cursing got me suspended in school I know that it would have the same affect on everyday life. Then I knew it was a sign to stop. I grew up believing that it was ok to curse because the people that I was around did it. If I never gained the knowledge that if you change your mind it'll change your life, there's no telling what I would have got into.

We are all sent signs from God. Most of us refuse to take action on them. He always sent some type of sign whether what I was doing was right or wrong. My daily activities are positive so I know that I must be doing something right. After the break up, I began to write

down my feelings, page after page after page. I didn't take seriously what I had written until I read it to myself. I noticed how in high school I had a passion for writing. I noticed that in English class we would always be assigned an essay and most of my classmates' essays were 250 words maximum. I would write at least 400 words. I would simply write whatever came to mind, it always made sense to me. I noticed how I always had more to say than the average writer. I began to look at motivational videos that would help me find success. I was blessed by
God to be happy again. I still needed something to capitalized my talents on. Les Brown once said a bible phrase For where your treasure is, there will your heart be also.-Matthew 6:21. So, to me, that meant to continue what I love doing until I see improvement. There were many things I loved to do like playing my video games, making people laugh and simply writing. I needed something that would push me to my next level of success. I knew for a fact that playing my video games wouldn't make me successful. My mom would always preach to me about how I can't get nothing done when I focus on the game. I also thought it was too late for me to become a comedian, my self-esteem was too low. I was afraid that people wouldn't take me seriously because I was just getting over a break-up. I was afraid of rejection from the crowd and I thought about everyone on social media trying to be a comedian. Many doubts were running through my head as to why I couldn't become a successful comedian. The last resort was writing.

Days went on and I continued writing my feelings down and watching motivational videos. Les Brown encouraged me to leave a mark in this world. Basically meaning whatever ever I want to put in the universe put it out there because it matters. Almost every motivational speaker I listen to says, "If being successful was easy everyone would do it." which made me realize whatever I was going to do would be hard. A thought came to mind that my writing had to become a novel or a Lifetime movie. In high school I won the best sense of humor award which gave me the thought of being a comedian. I knew I had something special in me just because of the award.

Many of my friends at school believed in me when I didn't believe in myself. Many believed that I would be a motivational speaker because I always seemed to bolster people's confidence, whether it was when we played basketball or by telling them right from wrong. I was an optimist without even noticing. I always saw it as a win a situation no matter what needed to be done.

Early in life when I would research the mind, one thing that caught my attention was that you have to win in your mind before you win in life. This pushed me to another state of realization that I can be successful. I
needed more confirmation on successful people so I continued to listen to Big Sean's Hall of Fame album. I had already known that everyone was birthed just like me which made believe that if they can become successful I can too.

Chapter 3

Signs and Confirmation That Being Successful Was Possible

On my road to success I began thinking about how we are all here for a purpose. Most of us change the world, most change people lives, and most love the living of life. I use to wonder why most people don't realize how beautiful they can make their own lives by challenging themselves. I noticed how many of my family members seemed to lack certain knowledge that they acquired when they were young. Many of them talked to me about how they wish they could've gone back to a young age and start their lives all over again. Basically, many regretted the situation they were in and they felt as if they ruined their lives. By their mentoring me, their mistakes in life made me become more ambitious about going down the right road. Many people told me how I still have time to mess up in life. I knew it was nothing but negative talk, I realized how risky life was when you're doing wrong thing, so I refuse to listen and continued doing the right thing. I told many of them how it's still possible for them change their mind, which will eventually change their lives. They didn't take me seriously, because I had nothing but knowledge to show for it. We only get one chance at this thing we called life. I thought about all the things I wanted to accomplish which were my dreams and all the things that I wanted to experience. At a young age I always wondered when I would get a chance to do the things my mom wasn't able to do and be financially able to get the things that I wanted. We always had to ask family members for help. I didn't get a chance to get exactly what I wanted until I got a job. I figured I'd have to work my whole life to get what I wanted. I was told that either you're going work on your feet or sit at a desk. Of course, I thought about the desk, but I knew I had to crawl before I walked. I had a good work ethnic and OCD (obsessive cleaning disorder) to keep me going.

Being a hard worker was natural to me, so whenever I saw someone who was lazy or sloppy I'd get offended. My grandma always fussed at me about being neat. I had to come to realize that most people weren't brought up like me, most of us were raised differently. I began to visualize being a boss before I made it. I had to instill it in my mind so, when I made it I wouldn't settle for less. My inspiration came from those artists who were signed to a record company and once they built up their buzz they started their own labels, becoming their own boss. For example, I remember watching Words of Wisdom on Youtube and I watched Rick Ross say how ambitious he was. They showed a video of him telling us exactly what his future was going to be. He was showing his tattoos before he made it in the industry. The tattoos were explaining how he knew he was going to get what he deserved. I noticed how he explained the law of attraction. He said many things that caught my attention, one was how it's best to start from the bottom and work your way up. I started my LMAO business from the bottom so this encouraged me. Then Rick Ross said that you have to work harder than everyone around you. I already knew I was a hard worker, so I prayed to God and asked Him to work harder on me than He was, because I was striving for the best.

I gave up on social media when I began to travel my road to success. I knew if I had stayed there I would never get the mindset of a truly successful person. I think of social media as something to use when you compare yourself to others.

I was chasing my dream, I was listening to music, or watching motivational speaker videos. They both had me thinking more. I thought about playing my game and talking to friends but it wasn't worth it, whenever I began to mention my dreams to my friends they tended to laugh at me. Many of them still think it's impossible to become successful. Big Sean opened my eyes and broke down how to become a successful man. After that I listened to the entire Hall of Fame album. His lyrics became more realistic to me. I was so hungry for knowledge at the time. I was on my road to success before I pass it up. I watched a movie called, "The Secret" which is a film consisting of a series of interviews demonstrating The Law of Attraction. At the time I first saw it I thought it was too long and I refused to watch it. I had no knowledge then, but I was determined to watch it and I wrote down every powerful thing they said in my journal, I didn't want to miss anything.

I started ignoring the things that I knew would kill my dreams. Anything can distract us which makes us lose focus on what's important… "our dreams." I began to think about how social media is like a lust to certain people. Many may lust for relationship goals, luxuries, drugs, celebrities and many other things. On my road to success I stopped getting on social media because I knew I'll fall in a trap and get distracted. My situation was that my girl left me and her new boyfriend began posting pictures of them on the site. I thought about commenting on the photos until I came to my senses. I knew that it would make me look bad if I was to comment on what I saw. If someone takes your girlfriend many think that you were a fool to let her go. I didn't want to be criticized, so I tweeted I won't be back on here until I get the satisfaction that I was looking for. I made an oath to myself no one but she and her new guy would know why I posted it.

Chapter 4

Learning From Reminiscing On The Past

I sometimes get confused by how most people believe in God and what God gave them but don't believe the promises God made to them. T.D. Jakes said, "It's not enough to believe in God if you don't believe in yourself." I used to ask myself, "How am I going to make it if I ever hate on someone else 's dreams?" When I first believed it was possible for me to become an author I took it seriously and was getting all kinds of compliments. When I got older I was making God smile on me. I looked at this generation and saw how they were talking about people who were already successful. I have more blessings than others that I really need to be thankful for. I thought, "When I become successful will I have people who dislike me as they do others, or would they hate on me like the others do?" I knew it was a yes for sure because people nowadays make hating a habit. I'm so happy that we have a God that never changes, He is always the same. Some people take God for granted and continue to do negative things. Yeah I know we aren't perfect but we can change by not always blasting negative things about other people on the internet. Growing up I wasn't taught anything about hating or disliking others, it was all common sense to me not to hate and it brought me a long way.

On my road to success I began to think about all the history and the legacies that were left to my generation. I began to think about Dr. Martin Luther King Jr., how he taught us to dream. I'm very thankful for him because if he didn't tell us about dreams, who would have? That's confirmation on why I believe that everything

happens for a reason. I actually believe that I can be anything when I think about all of the celebrities we look up to now. Sometimes I wonder how are they are able to chase their dreams and make it. I can do it too! I was already smart enough to know most had to work hard to get where they are now. I believe if I continue to put God first I'll be up next for my blessing. It seemed to be common sense to me that one day I'll be successful. I just wanted it more than it wanted me. I seemed to slow down and balance it
out which means for me to learn as much as I can about what I'm chasing after. Then it'll inspire me more and more to stay focused on what it was that I want. It came true. I always had the mindset that if I do something good and I get a good result out of it, I'll work every time. My mindset became one to grow more and more just from my belief that I was put on this earth for a reason, and for a GOOD reason. God isn't done with me yet I know that He has great things in store for me throughout my success.

Beware of those who are there when you are on your road to success. If they really believe in you they'll want better for you at all times. My experience with those who began to come around when I was on my road for success was that they only wanted what they could get out of me. It was crazy how when I began to act how I used to act, which was being broke not chasing my dreams that they weren't as interested in being around as they were before. I knew chasing my dreams and minding other people's business really didn't go together. I often heard the phrase, "the harder the struggle, the sweeter the success." I didn't believe it but now I realize how true it is. Most of my friends expected me to make them laugh whenever they call me or get in touch with me. No matter what, I know that success is in my mind and my heart. I have no time to play when I become successful. Many say the I've changed but I noticed how I changed for the better. Many refuse to take challenges on changing themselves because they may feel like they're going to be judged. I remember how my grandma always told me people disliked Jesus so my conscious made it clear to me that I shouldn't have a worry nor thought about what others have to say about me. It made my relationship stronger with God by noticing I made a change in my life and I can continue if I stop caring how others feel about me.

One thing I noticed was the need to watch certain people. Most only use you for their convenience. On my road to success, I started to think that it was because of the way I began to act. Many didn't have vision
like I did, they always thought I was "doing the most" as they call it. I honestly think no one saw how possible success was when I was coming up. I noticed how certain people would call me anytime they needed money. I wasn't stingy, I gave it because I thought I was doing the right thing. I always believed that it would come back to me, it was just a matter of time. As more people began to take advantage of me, my mom noticed and she questioned me why I'm taking so much money out of my account. I told her the reason then she began to fuss at me about how people will continue to use you if you let them. It really hit me when I thought about my future, I thought about when I become rich they'll literally rob me blind without me even noticing it. I'm thankful for my mother letting me know what folks will do to you when they think you don't know what's going on around you. Many would've fussed with their parents or whomever would have told them to stop letting people take advantage of them. I feel that was a warning before destruction. I looked at life now like God won't fail me. Things would have been quite different if I wouldn't have listened to my mother and had learned the hard way. I'm very grateful for the positive people that I have in my life, because I know one thing, if it had not been for the Lord on my side I don't know where I would be!

It's best you walk alone when you are on your way to success, I've watched people walk in and out of my life on my road to success. Many thought I was boring or lame because all I talked about was my future. I saw it all, my vision was clear, I envisioned myself happy. I stayed with the mindset that I grew and refused to let drugs or alcohol destroy my vision. When God blessed me with the mindset I have now, I remained focused. Many said I was "doing the most" by dreaming too much or that I was over thinking. I honestly think that none of those whom I grew up with had a positive vision of the future. I always dreamed about having a group of people who think like me and have the same vision as me. I couldn't change any of my friends' mindsets because they might have looked at me as though I didn't practice what I preached. I know we all make mistakes constantly, but I feel like if you keep making the same mistake things will get ugly in the end. I've learned to surround myself with people who want more out of life. I now have no fear or doubt that God will lead the right people into my life again.

Chapter 5

Mentor Guidance

I was once told to eat the meat and throw away the bone. I was given this quote by my mentor, it was really helpful when I thought about it and took action on it. My mentor was basically explaining how most people aren't Godly but you gain knowledge from anyone. He said it was a must that I shift because I had to know what was Godly and what wasn't and that most ungodly people have some knowledge that I can still learn from them. The most important was that you can't "unhear" something. That's why I needed the shift I began thinking about things he told me and I started watching certain celebrities' interviews. I took all the knowledge that inspired me and made the best of them like, when they said now we have to give back to our communities once we've made it. I let all the inspiration sink in and used my vision of what I wanted. I noticed how many people my age were infatuated with celebrity altercations. Well, I wasn't, because I know they were either playing or just doing it for nothing. It was a lot of altercations. It was a lot of different mess going on with them. I paid no attention because I couldn't learn anything from it. I wanted more inspiration than entertainment. I refused to give my attention to any negativity, I knew there was always something better I could've been doing or even reading about.

Nothing is bad or good but thinking makes it so. On my road to success I began to think about all the wrong that was done to me, how most people took my kindness for weakness and all the wrong I did in life. I began to think that my life was cursed because of my past. I wasn't aware of what I use to say and I noticed how that affect-

ed me the most. I thought about how I used to joke with my friends all the time or make jokes about them. I feel like since God knew I was doing wrong he just sat back and watched and when I began to do something right there would be an obstacle stopping me, so I went back to doing wrong. Joking on others became a habit to me every time I told a joke or said
something people always would laugh at the things I would say. That's where I got my idea from thinking one day I would become a comedian. I gave up on it when I thought I wasn't funny enough. Over time I gave up on being a comedian but a guy I used to joke around with is now making lots of money by creating social media videos. I began to think about how he had the mind and heart to do it. I realized he just believed in himself, which I didn't. I noticed how he didn't care about criticism, which I did. I was worried about being talked about, but over time I've learned life's lesson from situations, like not caring about what others say or even think about me. As long as I was doing what I knew was right and positive in God's eyes, I was content.

So I began looking for answers in my life. I knew I wanted to change and become a better person for myself. My change at one point of time was to learn how to get over a girl who once held my heart in her hands. I had been with her for a long time. I got my answers from a lot of people, many told me to just start smoking. I looked on the internet and they said just move on with my life which was so true. I had to suffer with seeing her on the internet with another guy over the summer. I was shook until I was afraid to go on the internet because many people knew I just got out of that relationship. I knew that no one wanted me, at least that's what I thought. I was stuck, depressed and miserable. I caught myself crying then I remembered just falling to my knees and went to God. I knew He was always on my side I just never went to Him. I got on Youtube to listened to music that dealt with the situation I was going through. I found no one, but the one song that kept me was by Mary Mary "Thank You." The lyrics explained how she was lonely and God came comforted her. I knew how happy He was when she said it.

Then I stopped ducking those difficult things that kept me bonded. I had to man up and just let some people walk out my life even though I really wanted them in it. We should all know that everything happens for a reason. I wondered why people left me when I was on my road to success. Sometimes I would have thoughts as to where I began to second guess myself. As time went on I asked God to help me master my passion which were my dreams and goals that I was striving for. I
thought about the law of attraction which makes negatives turn into positives. I overcame people doubting me just by going to God and letting Him solve all my problems. I let those who disliked me become my motivation. I imagined how putting my book online, explaining how I got over certain situations in my life would help others.

I made a massive change while traveling on my road to success. I knew in order to maintain my focus I needed to keep it real with myself and others. I learned that if I want success for real I have to go get it. I knew my brain needed more work so I began to work on it myself by reading more and paying attention to the things that were going on around me. I started reading a book by Joyce Meyers, her book has taught me a lot more about life. It all was confirmation to what I've been prophesizing to my peers. I always preached about how it was possible for you chase your dreams. I had always known I'd eventually make it I just had to build up my faith and I knew it would take hard work. I thought I wasn't ready, I still needed a little more time to play. I got into more trouble after I realized I could've been doing better . I always heard that God won't fault you for what you don't know. Now since I have the knowledge that my mistakes really mean something to me I always talk to my friends about doing the right thing. I wasn't practicing what I was preaching and it began to affect my life.

Chapter 6

Deep Knowledge From Others

I often heard the saying that life is as hard as you make it. I noticed the situations I was in were all because of me, the place I worked, the people in my life, and the environment I stayed in. On my road to success I realized how much I affected my future by the decisions that I made. It was all due to the lack of knowledge that I had at that time when I was in school. I heard from Les Brown if you want what you have keep doing what you are doing this seemed like common sense to me. I just needed to change my life around. I wondered why I couldn't focus in high school and every time I attempted to do something hard I gave up and made an excuse saying we weren't taught that. Some people agreed with me and others didn't. The ones that didn't agree with me were always the ones to pass the class, not because they thought my excuse was stupid or ignorant it's just they were mentally better than me. They were taught not to give up when obstacles came their way. I wanted to be smart just like them. I thought my school life was all messed up. I once had a bet that no one would ever take me seriously because I was a class clown. I knew if I stopped making people laugh I'd feel like I had changed. I also heard that there's a time to play and a time to be serious. I knew that in class is where I needed to be focused and I couldn't joke around. It took my being stressed out about a girl for me to stay quiet and focus on what I needed to do. I had to stay and make up for a lot of class that I missed out on by joking around. I figured out something about myself, the ugly truth that whenever someone hurt me emotionally, I would try my hardest to make them regret what they did to me. Over time I kept being hurt emotionally and I learned how much power I had over myself. This made me think I had a passion for making people regret hurting me through my work ethics. So now my family, friends, fans and even my haters can not stop me.

On my road to success I took very seriously 4 keys to this thing we call life, health, wealth, love, and happiness. I was focused on happiness
and staying healthy. Many people in my family have diabetes and I knew if I continued putting certain foods in my body I'd one day have it to. I heard about all the symptoms and I did research and they all frightened me. I read that you can go into a coma which I feared the most. I knew one day I'll have to go but I didn't want to die from a situation I knew was avoidable. Now that I love myself more and care about my health I just think before I take such crazy actions. I went up against two choices, either do right or wrong. As for me, I choose to do the right thing, be safe and live my life. This obstacle taught me more and more about self discipline. I thought about how on my road to success I tried my best to write notes of my phone. I knew one day it would be valuable to me. I also worked on my health by doing pushups after every match I played on the game. I always played UFC,I also would shadow box in my room. When I play online matches of UFC many quotes will pop up one by one,Anderson Silva saying "a champion is defeated by his adversities he overcomes". This gave me confirmation that my hard work was gone to one day pay off. Another one of my favorites quotes is one that Jon Jones said, "the only limitations we have are the one that we put on ourselves". I don't believe in limiting myself but it took me a minute to man up to that one. I knew I was settling for less in certain situations. I knew I could do more and I knew that all things were possible if I only believed.

It's not about today it's about the future, where you are going. I had to realize that it's not about what you are going through at that moment. At the end of the day, all that matters is that you did your best in what you can do. I knew I was going to be successful when I stopped rushing it and I became patient. I started to enjoy my journey more and more. It felt good knowing I was working on myself and I was finally making a changes for the better. I now have the mindset that I'm really capable of doing anything, I just have to put my work in. Many fail at the new things that they try in life. I just pray to God and ask for guidance along my journey. My confidence is beyond the roof, it's a wonderful feeling when you know what it is that you want out of life.

I replaced hunger with happiness and, honestly, it's worth it. I used to become furious over the simplest things, and used to wonder would I have to work on it before it was too late. I thought about how most people one day feel great, then the next day feel down. I look at every attraction in life like that. Nowadays you may not know what the next person may have. One thing I've learned is to not have negative feelings. I had a vision which pushed my motivation to the next level. I reminisced and noticed that and instantly got on my grind to become successful. I learned and mastered the rules of the game. Be patient and willing to make it by always being positive. I didn't want negative thoughts coming up because I didn't want it to affect me. That's why I'm thankful that God led me down the right road. I have come to realize that I'm the chosen one. My grandmother always told me that before the age of 12 all of your sins fall on your parents then at the age of 12 they began to fall on you. At the age of 14, when I got into some serious trouble (to this day I regret that I made that mistake) and that sin fell on me. I always thought I was cool and God showed me something different. God knew my heart and he started sending me all kinds of signs to change my life around and I took action on them. I was in control of my heart. I always remembered important things people told me. They gave me knowledge that I wouldn't have learned from anyone else but them, they offered opportunities to change my life. I went through some situations again and again.

Some things you win, win, and win and there are some things that cause you to lose. This saying made me think about the best of both worlds. We all want to win and celebrate it. We also know that win-

ning makes you feel good, but when you win, you win and when you lose, you're wise. I never remember being labeled as a winner until I learned how to control my anger and stay focused on what it was I really wanted. I began to think about my future and wonder if I would let all the wins go to my head and control me. I noticed how the successful win and get theirs, which only pushed me to do better in life. I thought about how God would keep me in the winning category but if I lost, I knew it would have been for a reason. I try my best to learn for it and move on. I kept focusing on God by taking one day at a time. We as people need
to stop complaining about why we aren't successful and do everything in our power to become successful which is letting God know that you are ready to travel the road to success by first getting your mind right. I always asked myself, "Why don't I sound or even look like an author?" Then something hit me and said, "So, how does an author look?" I knew that I was serious about my dreams I just had to push forward to my goals. My self-esteem was boosted and I knew that one day that I would be in front of an audience speaking to them, telling them all about my success. I began doing things differently, like bettering myself and my character. It became a habit so I promised myself that I will always do positive things because the outcome makes me happy. When you are going through this thing called everyday life you will have all kinds of obstacles come your way but, they have helped me remain focused, build up my confidence, and now I'm able to help others with the knowledge I have gained along the way.

Stay focused through the struggle on your road to success. I began to think back on my mom's life and the situation she's in today. My mom is one of the kindest people I know. That's where I got my good heart from, the habit of doing things right, a bit of my fashion sense and more. Growing up, me and my mother's relationship was strong. Even though we were like friends, when I was wrong she would let me know. She has never accepted the wrong I've done. At that time I use to think that she was just being mean to me by always saying no when I asked her for certain things or to just even go hang out with the fellas in the neighborhood. Mom always knew the troubled ones and the good ones. It was okay for them to come to the house, but she never let me go out. I use to be really mad until my grandma hit me with the realization that one day I'd be killed hanging around those guys. I still wanted to hang around them just to be cool, most carried guns and stayed in a lot of trouble. I started to respect it because it all seemed true to me. I always heard the saying that you are who you hang around. So I began thinking about my situation. I didn't want to start carrying a gun nor start getting in trouble. I just hung around most of my friends just to make them laugh. I had no idea that I'd be introduced to trouble with them. She told me she prayed and prayed but I just wouldn't listen. I started realizing how much trouble I was engaging in and I wanted a change for myself. I heard many stories from my grandma about kids not listening to their parents and ending up dead or in jail. She instilled in me "warning comes before destruction". So I just avoided situations that I thought were bad. I had to stop hanging around certain friends that I was chilling with. I feared death but I knew that when I was by myself I had nothing to worry about, so as time went on being solo has taught me a life's lesson that my mom had been trying to explain all the while.

It's better to have faith than regret. I began to pay attention to all of the times I've failed was stupid and I basically just didn't know. My priorities were a bit messed up I missed out on life's lessons while playing around in high school. I noticed how I never attempted to focus back then. I used to live in the moment and think in the future. I've learned from E.T. and Les brown that nothing is easy because it's not supposed to be. I believe that we are made to challenge ourselves, we can succeed in the end even if we fail in the sot-term. We should try again and again, never giving up. Logic's music gave me confirmation in his song when he said, "We kept moving, assuming even the greatest fail too." This is true. That piece of wisdom has helped build up my belief system that I'm able to do anything I put my mind to. It takes focus to get exactly what it is you are striving for. If being successful were easy then everyone would be successful.

Then I thought about all the people we have in this world. The ones who don't challenge themselves to become successful simply fail and I didn't want to become a part of that crowd of people. I always told myself when I get there I will chase it all over again and never stop. All I ever thought about was me not going back to that place I once was when I broke down, I know if I stay consistent with what I'm doing everyday on my road to success I will achieve many things. I will eventually make it to where I've always wanted to be. It was hard to believe that I could write the next best seller or even better, become the next billionaire. I noticed how if I started to believe in the power of God all things were going to work for
the good of them that love the Lord. It is only in a matter of time until He will give me ten times what it was I asked Him for. Once I showed God that I was ready to accept all that I asked for He began to send me on my journey that would test my patience and I passed them all. I've asked for God's grace and mercy over my life and I believe He'll provide just what I asked Him for. I believe that people can tell you the most motivational things but if you don't take action it was just a waste of time. Every positive experience that I believed would make me better, I took action on… now I can't be stopped.

A set back is merely a setup for success. I always looked at the artist Lil' Boosie for instance, he was incarcerated for 6 years and now he's home. God has forgiven him and he noticed. I don't know much about his story but I do know that he hasn't given up on his dream. I honestly think that he's doing better than he was before. There are many rappers that would've experienced what he went through and would've given up on life. I noticed how he had all the songs that made me open my eyes before he went to jail. He made so many wonderful songs. One for instance, is "Never Give Up," when he was in jail I said he's going to come home and do it big. He also has a song called, "Take That Pain Away." It really moved me and motivated me. The whole time he was in prison I said I know he won't give up, I knew he would come home and go to work on his music career again. I know that God has something for each and every one of us whether we are right or wrong because we are all his children.

It doesn't take money for you to get your mind right, its up to you. I've mastered the mindset of being hungry for money, I eventually got over financial issues. When I got my first job I noticed how material things didn't matter to me anymore. Every time I got paid I'd put my money in the bank. I figured out how to manage my money. I was always told that when I make it I'll be a wealthy man because it so easy to get money nowadays. I didn't blow my money, so that was one advantage that I had. I always told myself as long as my shoes are clean I'll be

okay. I was once told that my dad was a well groomed fellow. I grew up believing I was a neat person and that I was well groomed also. I knew my mom wasn't able to afford $200 shoes for me and my baby sister. I just settled for a descent pair of kicks for the both of us, which I took care of as if they were the price that she couldn't afford, I was a very grateful child coming up in this world. As I got older I was able to get more and more shoes that filled my closet to the ceiling.

Chapter 7

On My Road to Success

On my road to success I thought about what really was ahead of me and how should I handle the obstacles. I had people in my life who I began to blame for my destiny, which was my fault. Whenever I had it in my mind to hurt those who tried to kill my dreams I began to think about karma. I knew whatever I do to someone will come back on me even worse than I thought or could imagine. I was told by my mentor that when God created heaven and earth He made karma a law , you reap what you sow. I began to think about how well I treated people and how I was always willing to give them my last. I could do better and focus on my dream. It was a test when negative people tried to kill my dreams. I already knew how to overcome it. I wondered how most people let their anger overtake them when they found out that people were hating on them. Some kill and most let their haters be their motivators. I know that everything happens for a reason. If someone is hating on you, then you must be doing something right! You must be doing something good, which is doing what God has ordained you to do. This wisdom makes me think about T.D. Jakes when he said for every new level there is a new devil. But I stay on track by knowing God is more powerful than the devil and just knowing that he will be with me every step of the way and I know that I'll get to the next level. My dreams became a reality when I took the knowledge I got from others and let them motivate me and more. It was all making sense to me. There was nothing more important to me than my dream. I knew how much better I was taking care of myself. I didn't want anything to do with things that would jeopardize my future. I started ignoring my dreams killers more and more. I knew there was a "New Me." I was so proud of how much I had worked on myself. My work ethics started to increase and my whole attitude made a 180 degree turn. I heard someone say destiny has no expiration date on it. I've once read what you visualize about in your future will eventually come to pass. I'm a living testimony when it comes to this thing called life. I made my writing every night a habit, it was like a second job to me. At one point I began to think that I already made it, I just didn't get the prize yet. It is an amazing feeling to do what you said and it really comes to pass.

n my road to success I had to really work on noticing how distractions come easily. Earlier in my book I wrote on how becoming successful was easy. On most of my days I would get distracted by playing my video games. There was always this thought in my mind that I should be reading, gaining as much knowledge as I could. Playing my video game at night became a habit for me because that's when all my associates got online. I wasn't learning anything about my dream I was just wasting time. By writing a page every night I wasn't satisfied I knew I was able to do better so I got off my game and finished writing page after page. I had no girlfriend to talk to so my only choice was to continue chasing after my dream. I believe that hard work pays off. I thought about what if I put in all this work toward my dreams and they don't come true. I began to think of all the motivational speakers I've heard and how they said they came up. I wanted my day just like them, I noticed the long process was that most of them experienced, but everything worked out for them. Most of them had been criticized and talked about behind closed doors. My road was similar to theirs, but I bettered myself every time I was in their shoes. I didn't believe in violence because it was senseless to me. I knew it was going to be a cycle of violence going on. I've learned a lot from the law of attraction about anger. When I decided to change my anger and replacing it with happiness was very hard. I had no realization about how powerful God is so I learned on my own. It took a while, but I did believe if I knew how powerful He is I would have probably been a different person then. I don't regret learning how powerful and forgiving God is. There have been times I could've given up but as days went on I didn't attempt what the average person would have done. In high school I played a lot, skipped class and decided to shake back when it was time to graduate but it was too late then. I was still able to walk across the stage but during the summer when I decided to go fill out for college I wasn't able to start on time. I was very hurt I had my mind made up on what I wanted to go to school for and I did just that. All my plans failed I had nothing nor anyone to talk to. I didn't have a car to go to the library to work on the task that was assigned to me. So my mindset was still weak because I was getting over a breakup. I used to think that she was the only person that could make me happy. I had to start from rock bottom, and start a class on my own. She used to complete all of my work on the computer for me. All I had was God and myself when I was going through my state of depression. I thought about giving up because she was like my lifesaver when it came down to school work on the computer. I never did the work on my own she was always there for me. I thought about the consequences when I enrolled in college, I knew that she wouldn't be able to do the same for me then. I wanted to work at the chemical plant with my godfather. I knew I couldn't take care of my mom and sister if I started smoking again because I'd lose the job at the chemical plant. I needed income. I thought about my father being in jail and I didn't want to go down the same road as him. As I sat and thought about all of that, I got a job and I knew I was blessed. I started working at a restaurant called McAllister's Deli making $8.00 an hour. The minimum wage in Louisiana is $7.25 an hour. I was making $.75 cents more than the average teen. I was too blessed to give up. My mother was satisfied because I was helping her with my little sister. I wasn't a materialistic teenager, the only thing that excited me was progression. I also knew how this was my second chance at a positive life. At one point I quit my job but eventually I called them and asked for my job back and they rehired me, I knew it was nothing but the grace of God. I had no transportation to travel back and forth to work all the way to New Orleans. I remember lying on my boss and telling my aunt that my boss had put his hand in my face while yelling at me. This was my excuse to quit McAllister's. I only told her that because I couldn't get to the job

that I really wanted to work at, which was at the chemical plant. I thought that she might be my transportation. I was out of work for two months it really hit me when had no money coming in. My mom continued to fuss at me more to go and get my job back. I decided to call my boss and apologize to him for all the disagreements we had.

Chapter 8

Talking to Teen Audience

We now must take advantage of what we've been given, why not start now and take every opportunity to learn what we love doing? Why won't most of the us begin to test ourselves, if it's worth it? I first began to test myself by changing myself and it seemed very worthless to me at the time. I began to think that there was no meaning in what I was doing. I began to think about how it would be once I became successful. I was working on it and doubting myself at the same time. I realized how character wasn't built up by negative thinking. I've learned from Les Brown that we don't get old over time we get old because we don't take the time out to work on ourselves. I remember wasting so much time stressing because some disliked me, when I could've been reading how to get over it. That's why I'm thankful to be in this generation. Many fail to realize it but it's not as easy to become successful than it was back then. I believe it first takes knowledge to know what you are capable of and good at then go ask someone to help guide you through the process.

I honestly believe that it's so simple to obtain success nowadays because I think about all the technology we have and how we're able to look up anything we want. It'll explain how to do it. Sometimes I think about what if my mother had the opportunities that I have today. I think I would probably would have had a better experience at life than I did, especially my lifestyle back then. I now realize how everything happens for a reason. I noticed how God sat her down and made me the one in the family to achieve success. I know God didn't intend for my family to live like this. being miserable and unable to enjoy life as we should. I'm thankful that I found my Lord and Savior Jesus Christ. In my life I

learned how to balance what I thought was right to me. I knew it was Him that was teaching me the right way and things to do in life to become the successful one that I wanted to be. I learned pretty fast because I respect God and follow His rules like my life depends on it. I became a God-Fearing Man of God. As day by day passed I became more aware of the things I did and started seeking knowledge from those who were already successful. They taught me a lot and I now use those lessons to my advantage by learning from their mistakes and making the best of it.

I had an imaginary audience when I first start to write. I took advantage of my freedom, it was time we start being cautious about certain decisions I made. There are so many people in prison for life who wish to be freed, so many who want a second chance at life but they can't get it because of certain decisions they made. I saw many teens go down the same road that their fathers and mothers did. Many people choose the lifestyle that they have but it costs nothing to do the right thing and a whole lot to do wrong. I once was a victim of following in my father's footsteps but then God stepped in and whispered something in my ear and said, "My child, this is not the road that you want to take." It was crazy how I was doing everything my father used to do. My family members never approved of my smoking, it would literally upset them. I ignored what they told me because I always liked the way weed made me feel. I remember telling myself I know how to get rid of my problems and that was smoking to solve them, but it only made things worse. Every time that I smoked, I thought that I had the knowledge to do the things that I wanted to do. I thought that it strengthened my relationship with other people but it did nothing but burned out my brain. I always had the knowledge on how powerful God is. I was just living with a mindset that all bad things are supposed to happen to me.

Chapter 9

Obsessive Grinding

My grind became obsessive when I realized how much work I had to put into get where I wanted to go. I knew no one will get me there but the good Lord and my mindset to do right. It's a fact that I continue to work harder than I did in the last year. I wanted success so badly that I was writing and living my thoughts at the same time. I decided to take advantage of all the opportunities I had. I wanted to make each day worth it and I took no days off from doing it. Success was the only thing I was worried about. I started putting aside the things I really loved doing and stayed focused on my dreams. I started to think like Big Sean, he once said, "If I don't learn from the best I won't learn." I became infatuated with my own writing and inspirations. I knew I'd one day start to take my dreams seriously and it would pay off sooner than I thought. I realized how most people say it's too late and that's why I believe they aren't successful. Being young I knew to never doubt myself because of what people thought of me. I've seen some slacking on what they need to do, so I stepped in and spoke with them and explained to them that you have to put your best foot forward and move in the right direction and everything will work in your favor. I made sure that I encouraged them to be positive at all times.

On my road to success I began increasing my work ethics and responsibilities by remaining positive. I remembered my mother used to tell me when I was wasting time on my video game, "KJ you can't get nothing out of life while you're out of life while you are on that game." Which was true but my game was second nature to me. I had no vision for my future nor did I know what I wanted to do in life. Going outside was not an option for me because I wanted to play my game and stay out of harm's way. I stayed inside and that way I knew that no one in there would get me in any trouble. I'll never get in trouble that I can't get myself out of. M working took up a lot of my time, so it was work, then

home to the game. At one point I actually wanted to stop working just so I could rank #1 on the NBA status. I really wasn't serious about work, so my mother threatened me that she'd disconnect the internet if I didn't get my mind right. I talked back to my mom lots of times. I knew I was hurting her feelings but not knowing she would call my grandmother and my grandmother would fuss at me tell me I know better. For the most part, I paid no attention, but one thing she told me that made me think more was "The bible says "Honour thy father and thy mother: that thy days may be long upon the land which the LORD thy God giveth thee."" She would always say look at what happened to your cousin for not listening to me. My cousin was in jail for not making wise decisions. I did not want to be in jail nor dead, so I thought about how I would start to respect my mom. My mom would say, "Son, there are more important things in life than playing that game all day."

I knew she wanted me to focus on work rather than on the video game. So days passed by, work was kind of boring knowing my game wasn't important anymore. There was a guy at my job who was very passionate about working, so I asked him why he loved working almost every day. He said, "Young's, I have bills to pay and kids to feed." He said, "Always remember you're damned if you do and damned if you don't." That made sense to me and made me think about preparing myself for the world. I knew then that playing that game was not going to feed me and my family nor will it house me so I backed away from it for a while and only played when I had spare time.

My grind became obsessive when I really realized my actions and habits really affected my destiny. When I decided to get on my road to success I took being successful very seriously. I sometimes feared that I'd be distracted and go back to being the old me which was not a committed-to-self type, low self-esteem, heavy stress, and most of all smoking again. Working on myself and focusing on my destiny was a bit stressful because no matter how far I got I always felt like I was behind on my dreams. At one point I stopped telling others about my book, because most gave me a careless response. Sometimes it made me feel like it wasn't worth it. The only reason I continued chasing my dream was because when I looked back I knew then that God had pointed me in the right direction. I also thought about how I was born be successful and take care of my family. My life made sense to me when I looked back at everything I went through and looked at myself and saw who I had become in pursuit of my life. I knew how good I was to people which made me think everyone will support my book. I was a bit confused because everyone was anticipating the release date that I had given them. I didn't want to lie to them nor myself, so I always told them very soon. I really wanted a date but I couldn't find anyone to help me put it together.

Chapter 10

Primed for Success

Days before I knew I was going to really become successful I began to realize why God put me through the exact situations from the past all over again. They all made me who I am now. The waiting made me have more faith than ever in God. I started to understand more about life when my experiences and perspectives were in the right place. I was dream chasing without God at one point. I didn't get as far as I should have so I had no choice but to stay on Gods track. I learned in life how it's all about testing your faith when misery or depression hits you. I realized that it's better to live life to the fullest now. Also when depression hits, you begin regretting life and instantly lose faith in God. Many of us have different minds and our belief systems are very different. Many think God is not real and they wonder why God hasn't left His print or any proof, but He did, which is the bible. I believe that as generations went on it was written by other famous people and companies. I've learned from Les Brown that the bible is a motivational book, which is true because look at most of the people who are mentally and spiritually successful and most got there by believing in God. That's what made me believe that I can be successful. I tried and my dreams came true, of course if you choose to go your own way without God's guidance there is no telling what will happen to you in life. The bible teaches you everything that you need to know about life. If you are lazy and don't want to listen or react, of course, you'll lack in life's situations.

If you are not willing to take risks then you can't grow, and if you can't grow then you can't become your best, and if you can't become your best then you haven't chased your dreams to become successful or happy. You can only go as high and as far as you can see, and you can see as deep as you can go, but remember you can only dream as far as you can see.

On my road to success I remembered stressing if I would become the best bookseller there was. I always felt that people would read my book and enjoy it but I just was a little nervous. I don't have a college degree as of yet nor am I famous yet but I know one day I will become the greatest book seller there is. I wanted to become known by everyone in need of inspiration. I began thinking about how I would be able to get my book sold while I still worked at a restaurant. I began to think no one would take my book seriously with me growing up in the area that I did. When I was growing up I just put everything into perspective of what I loved doing. I began writing more and more that I started to question my thoughts. I started to ask myself if my fans would really be inspired by my writing. I still wanted my book to be perfect so I began gathering every thought that I could think of. With all the writing I still just wanted to be Kenneth (KJ), I just wanted my book to flow from the young to the old, throughout generations. I remembered trying my hardest to have all my grammar correct. I wanted to put words into my book that I'd recently learned. I also remembered getting a fortune cookie and it read, "Grasp everything around to achieve success in life." So after that I did exactly what I read. I remembered praying asking God to help me learn things that I've read along my journey. I thought I'd never find a way to be focused, now God has answered my prayers and I fell in love with learning different things. I began reading T.D. Jakes' book and he explained how God didn't create one to be better than the other one, I became afraid a bit because that's all I was worried about when I started writing. All the while I stayed calm and became the person God has ordained me to be. I learned to just be me and continue to write and speak to different generations about everyday life situations and how to "Learn More After Obstacles."

Made in the USA
Middletown, DE
28 June 2019